Dundalk Ontario in Photos, Saving Our History One Photo at a Time

Photography
by Barbara Raué
2012

Series Name:
Cruising Ontario

Book 10: Dundalk

Cover photo: Dundalk United Church, 200 Main Street

Series Name: Cruising Ontario

Book 1: London
Book 2: Dundas
Book 3: Hamilton
Book 4: Oakville
Book 5: Chesley
Book 6: Stoney Creek
Book 7: Waterdown
Book 8: Owen Sound
Book 9: Mount Forest
Book 10: Dundalk

Other Books by Barbara Raue

Coins and Gems

Arrows, Indians and Love

The Life and Times of Barbara
Volume 1: Inventions That Have Enhanced My Life
Volume 2: Entertainment That I Have Enjoyed
Volume 3: East Coast Trip 2009
Volume 4: Olympics
Volume 5: Wonders of the World

Dundalk Ontario

Dundalk (named after Dundalk, Ireland) is located in the southeast corner of Grey County. Dundalk services the surrounding agricultural area and also has a few manufacturing plants. Dundalk has the highest elevation of any populated place in southern Ontario at 1,735 feet (526 metres). Dundalk is located on Grey Road 9, off Highway 10. It is located northwest of Shelburne, and south of Markland on the way north to Owen Sound. Dundalk had regular passenger service on the CPR line, and freight trains moved grain, timber, produce and livestock to Toronto.

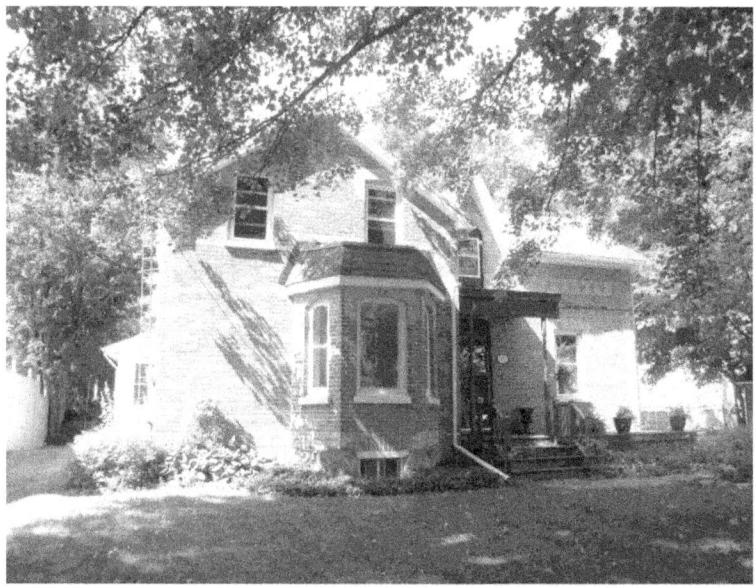

51 Osprey
Two-tone brick accents on the corners and below the eaves
Gothic style arches

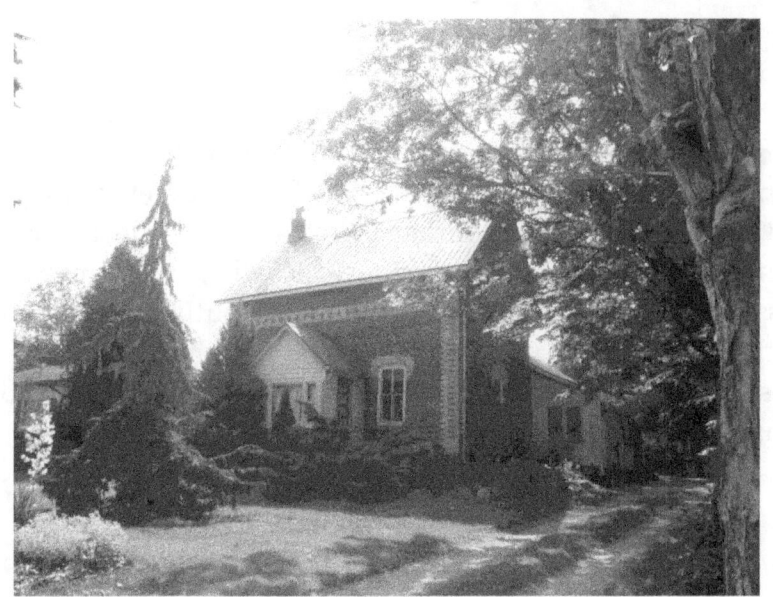

#545

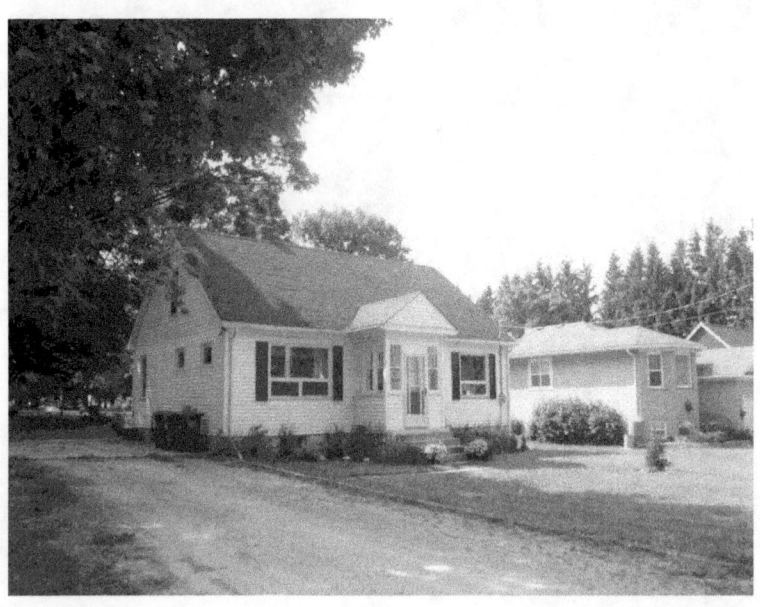

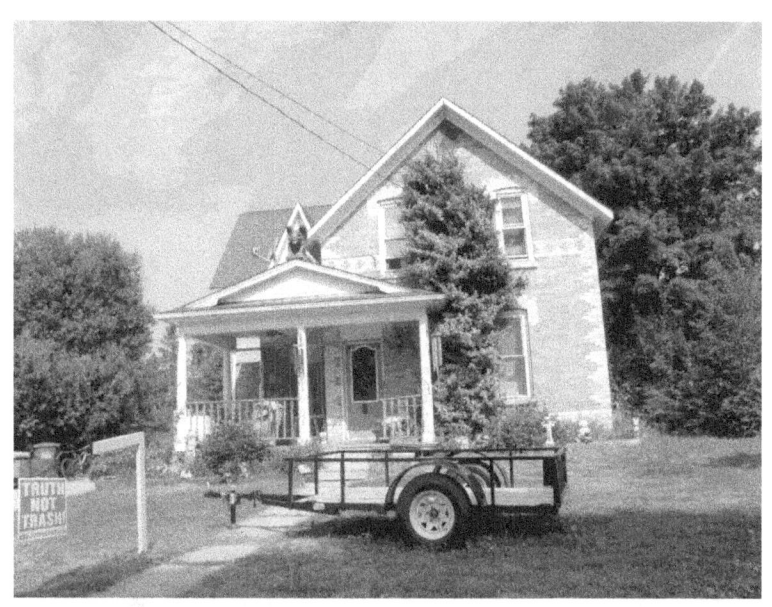

Two-tone brick accents

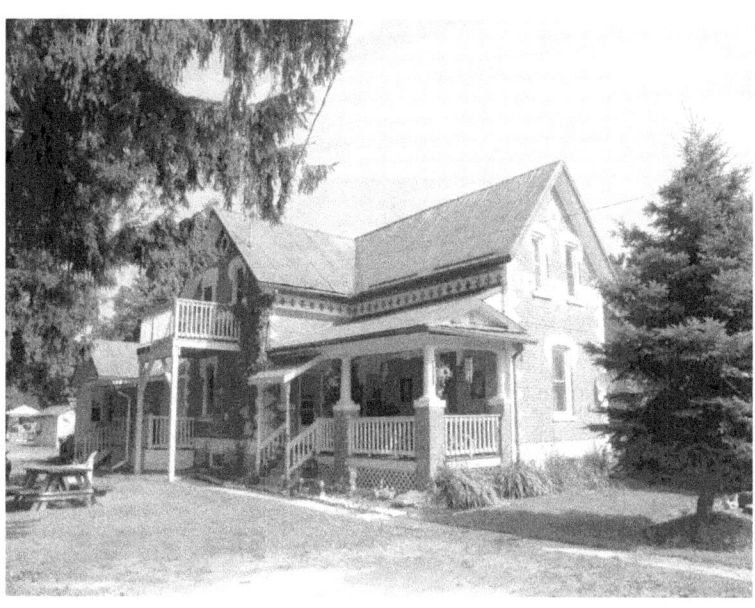

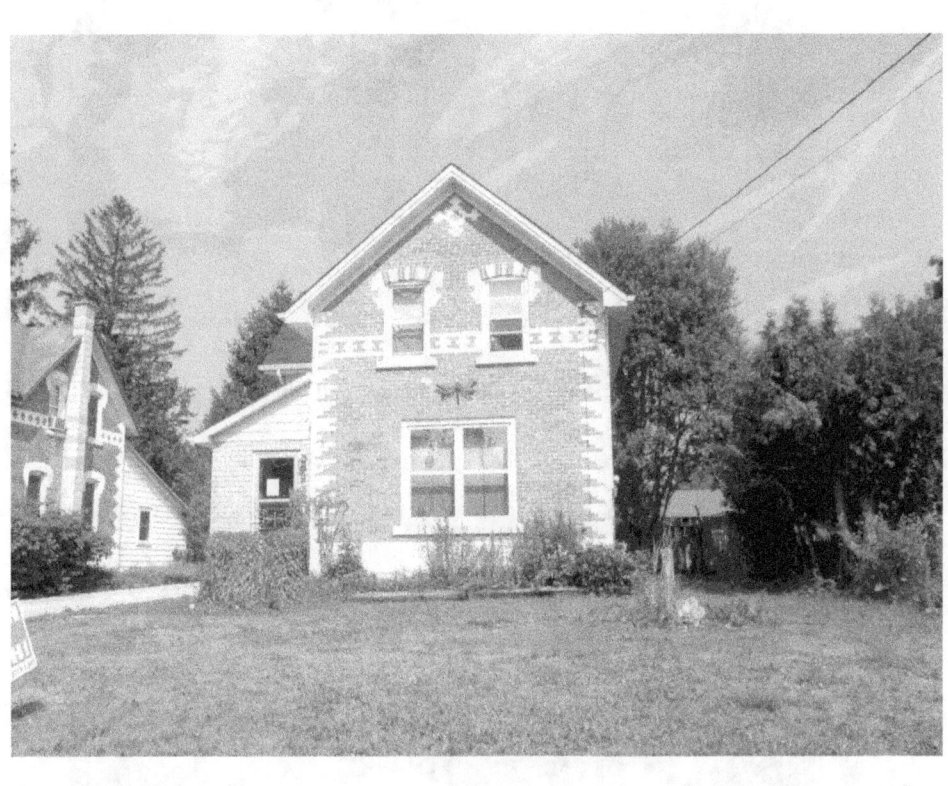

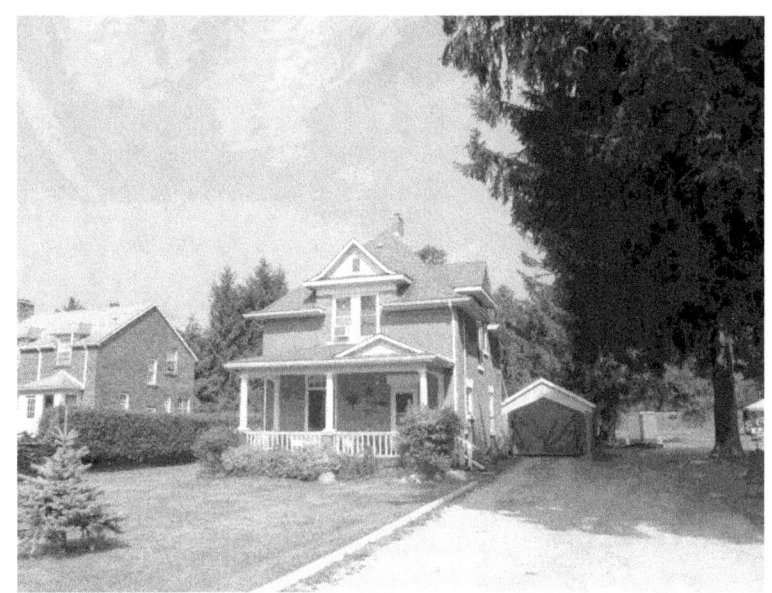

#442

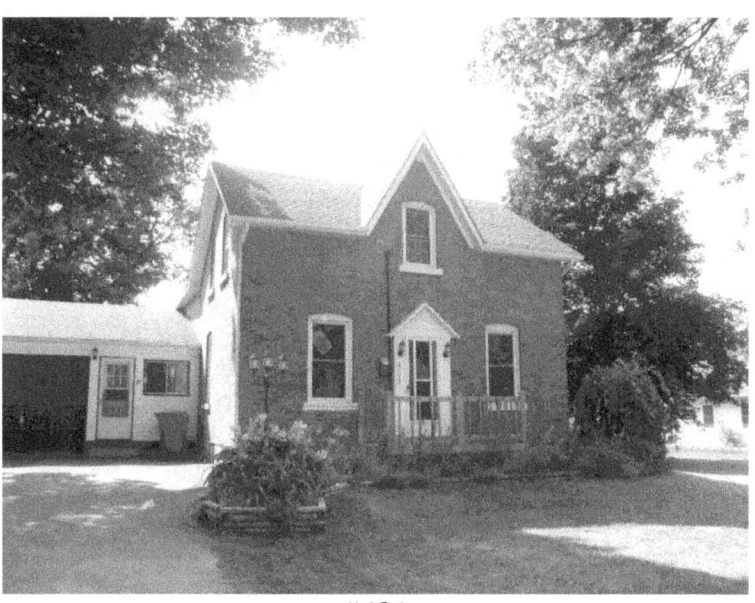

#421

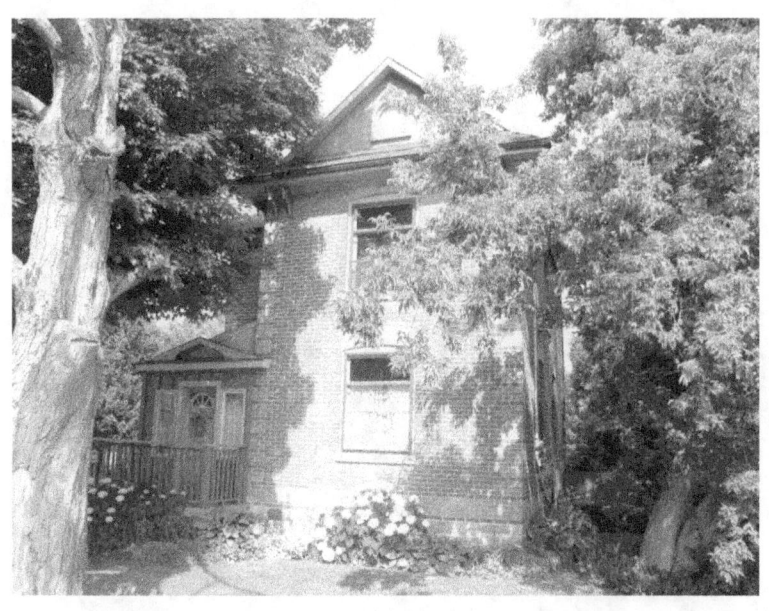

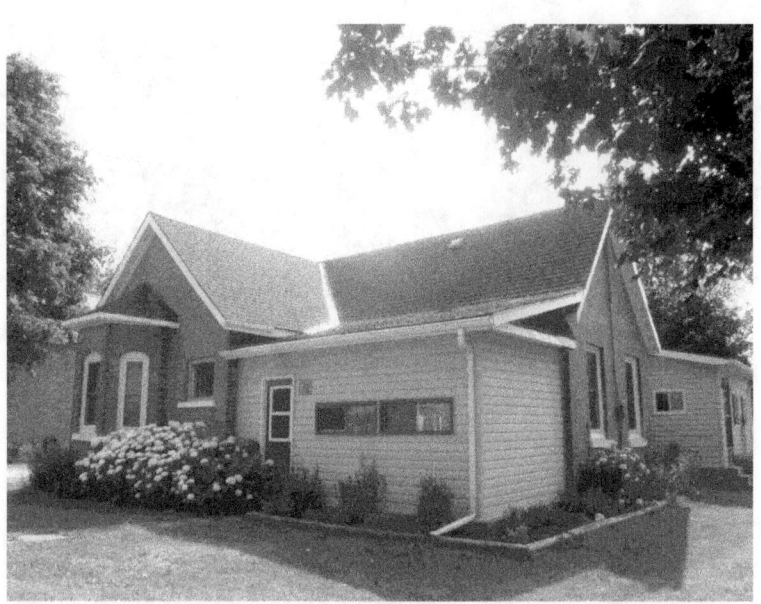

#351

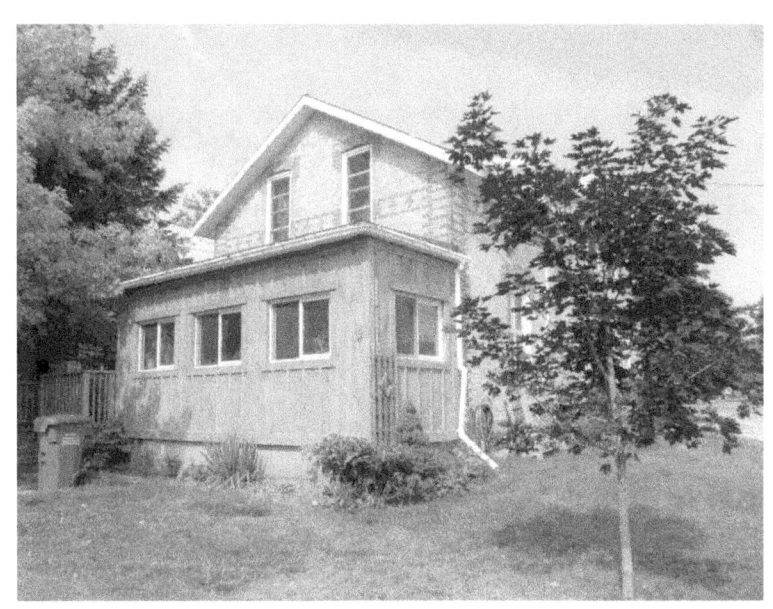

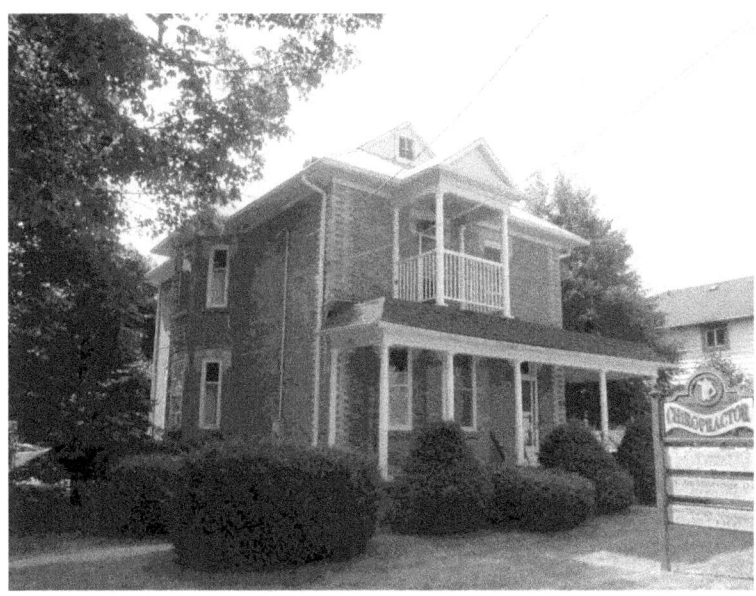

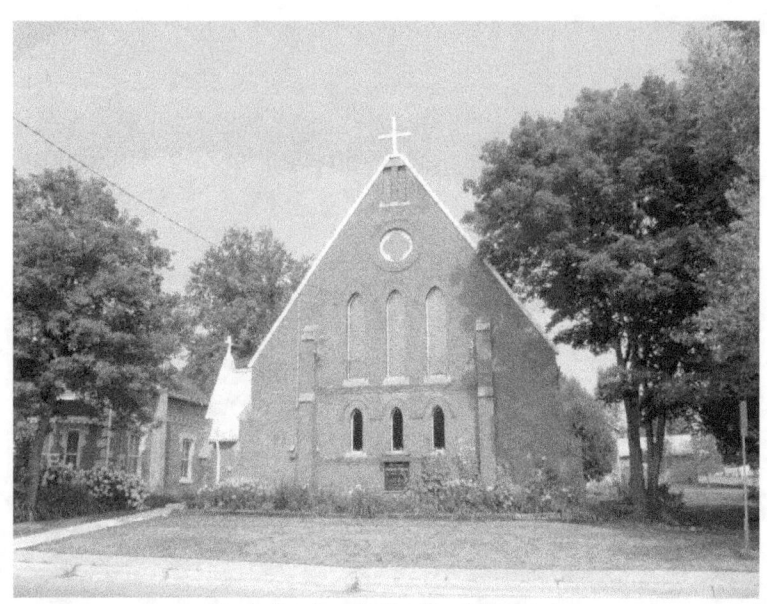

St. John's Catholic Church

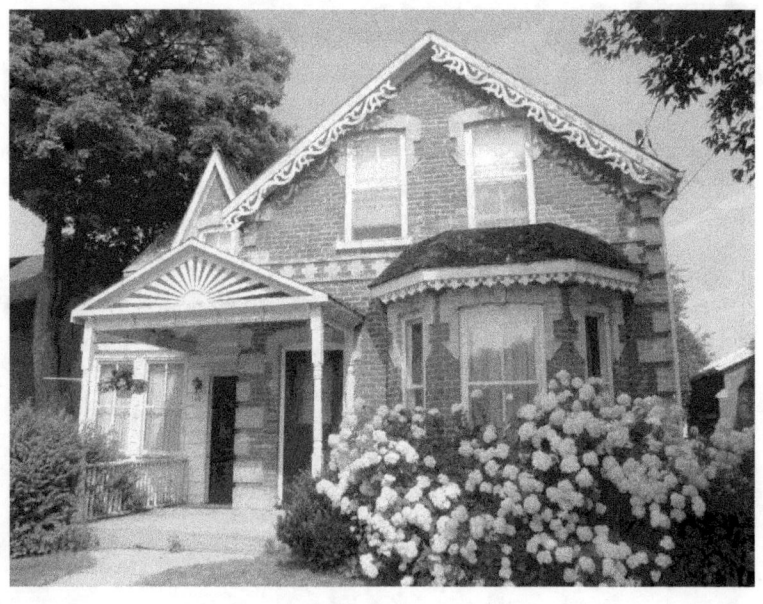

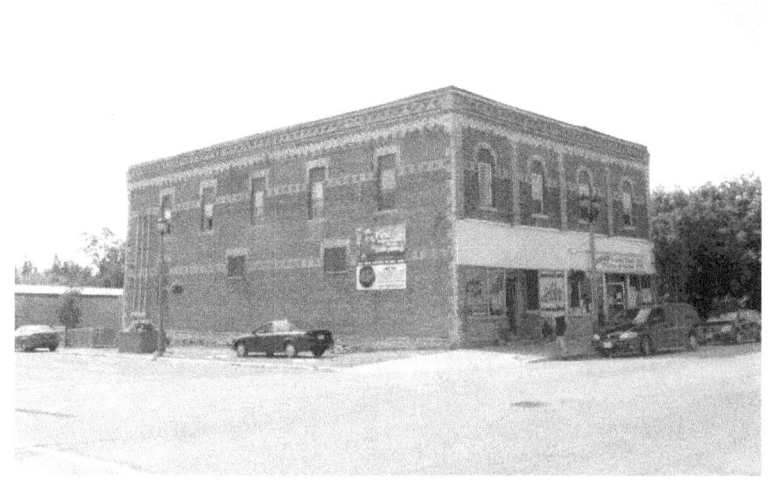

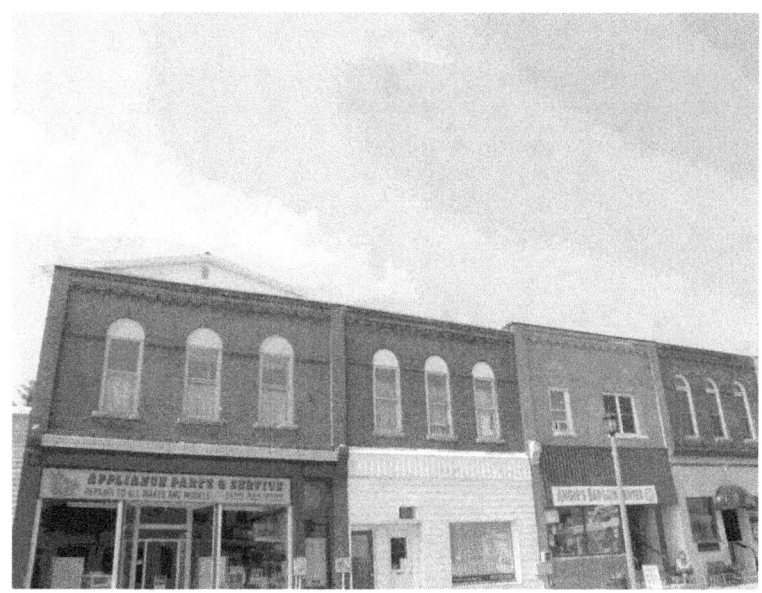

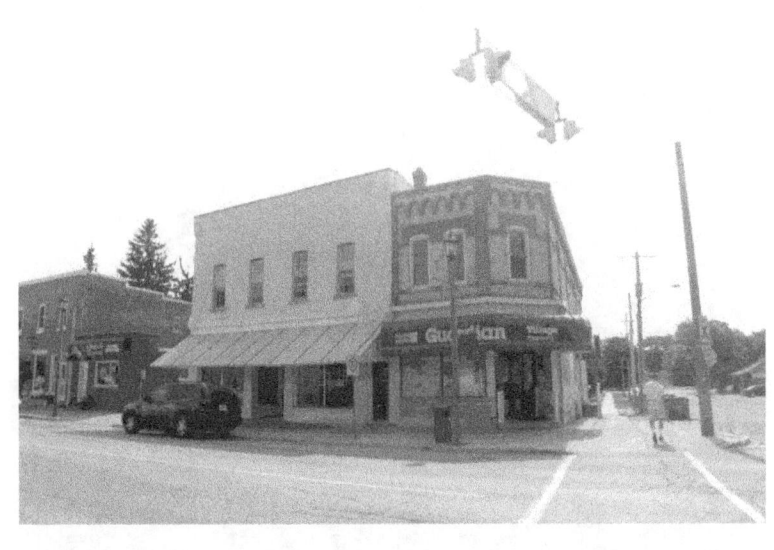

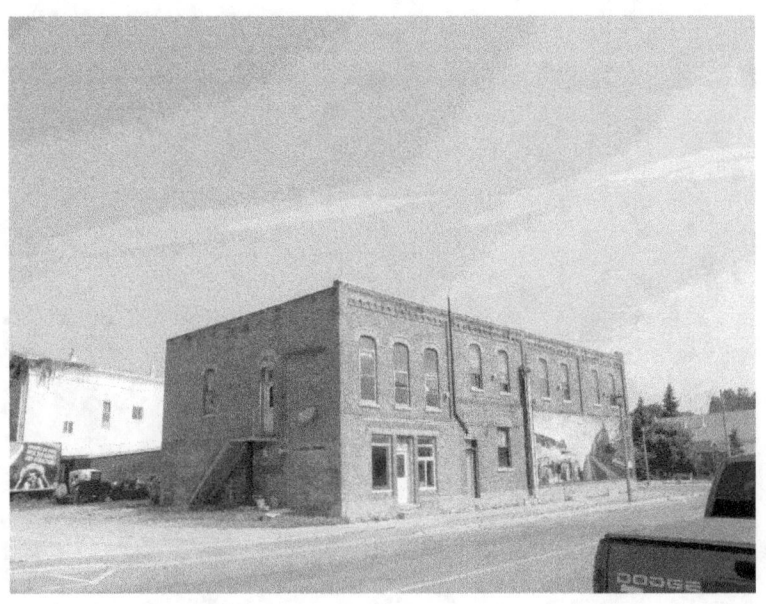

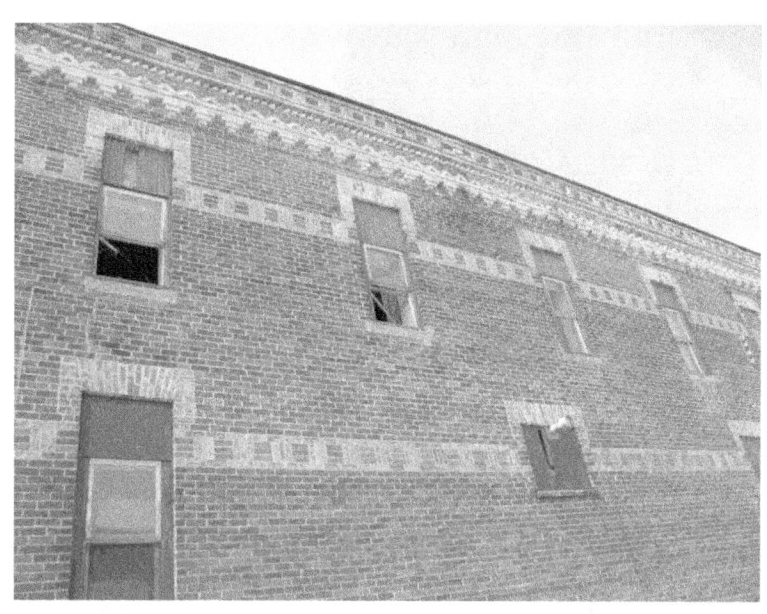

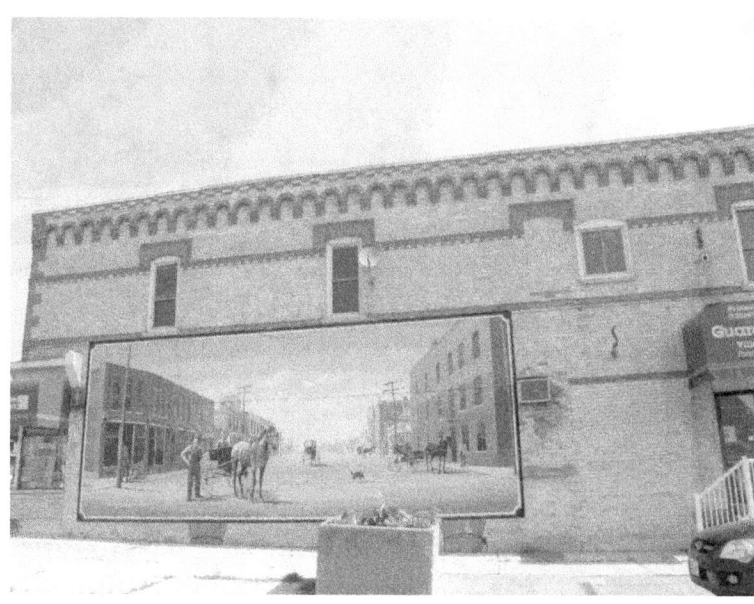

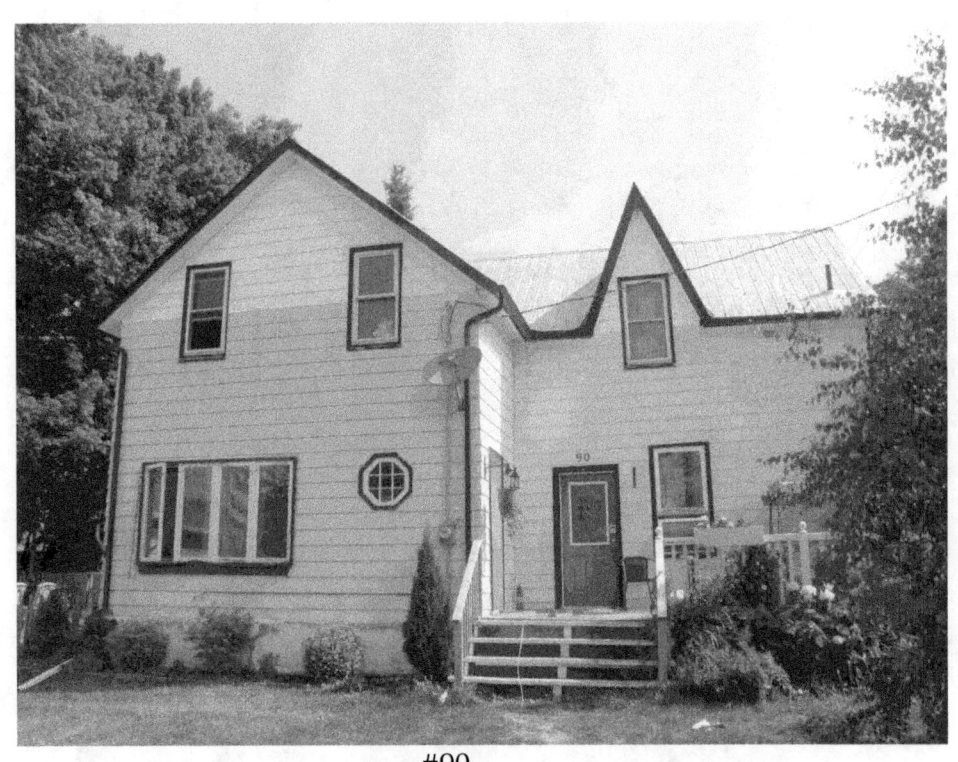

#90

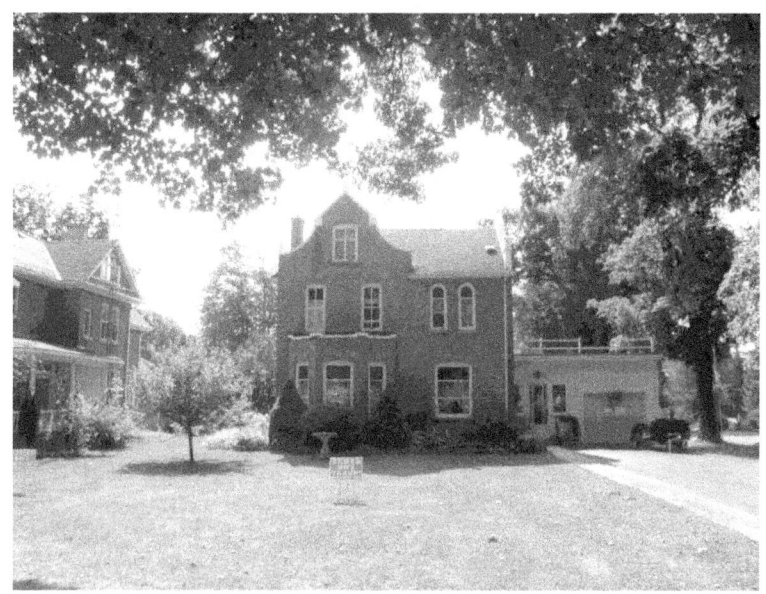

#91

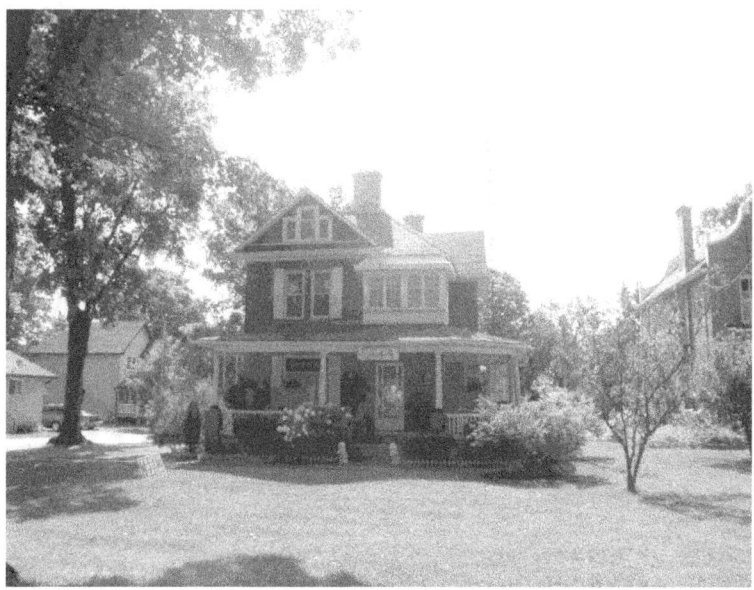

The Nicholls #97

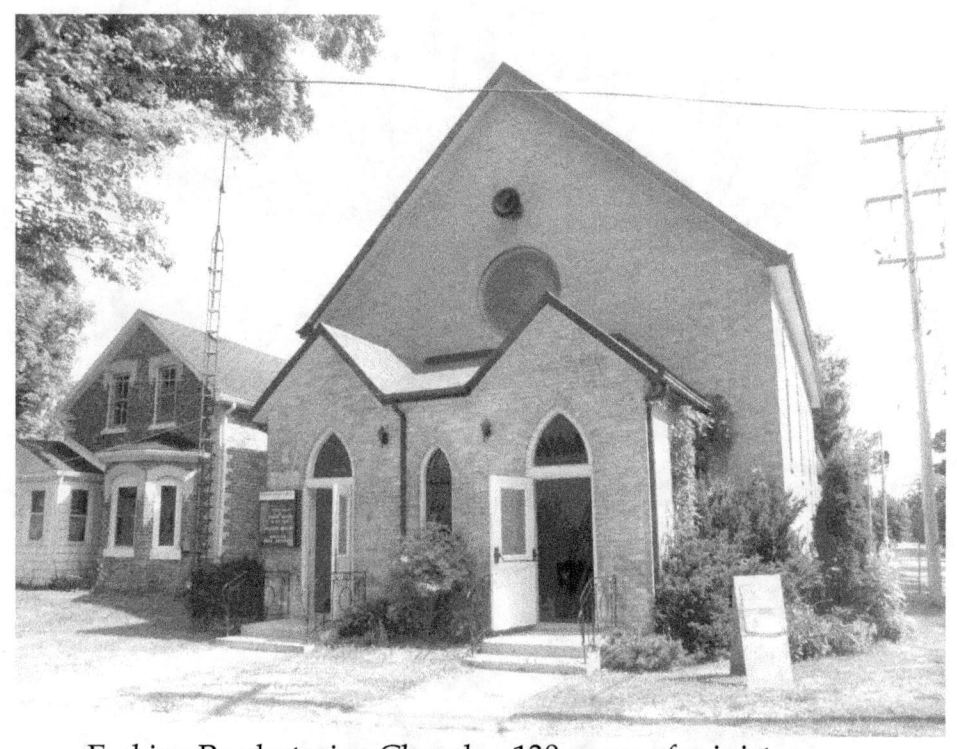

Erskine Presbyterian Church – 130 years of ministry
c. 1878 - 90 Artemesia South

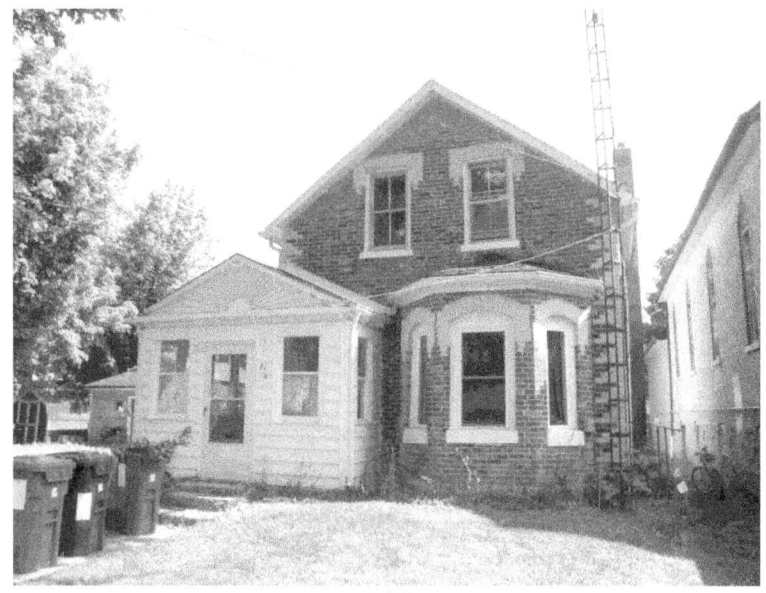

#80

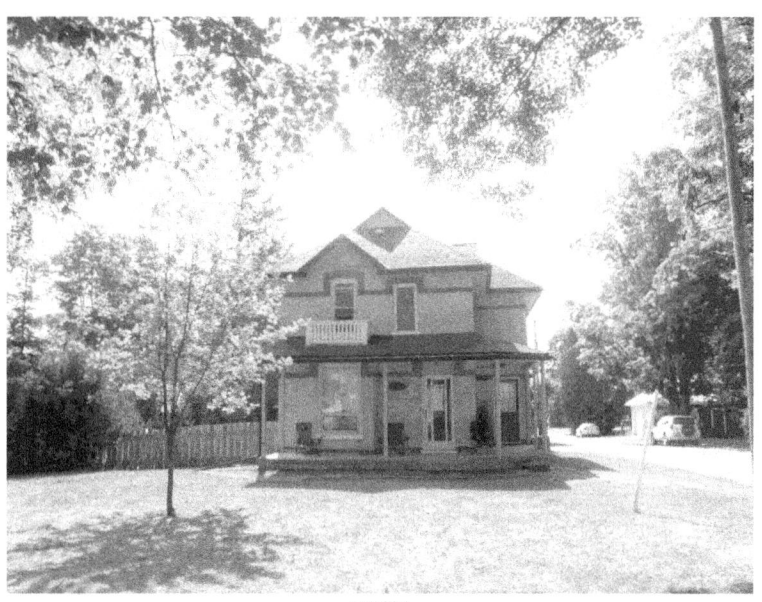

#151

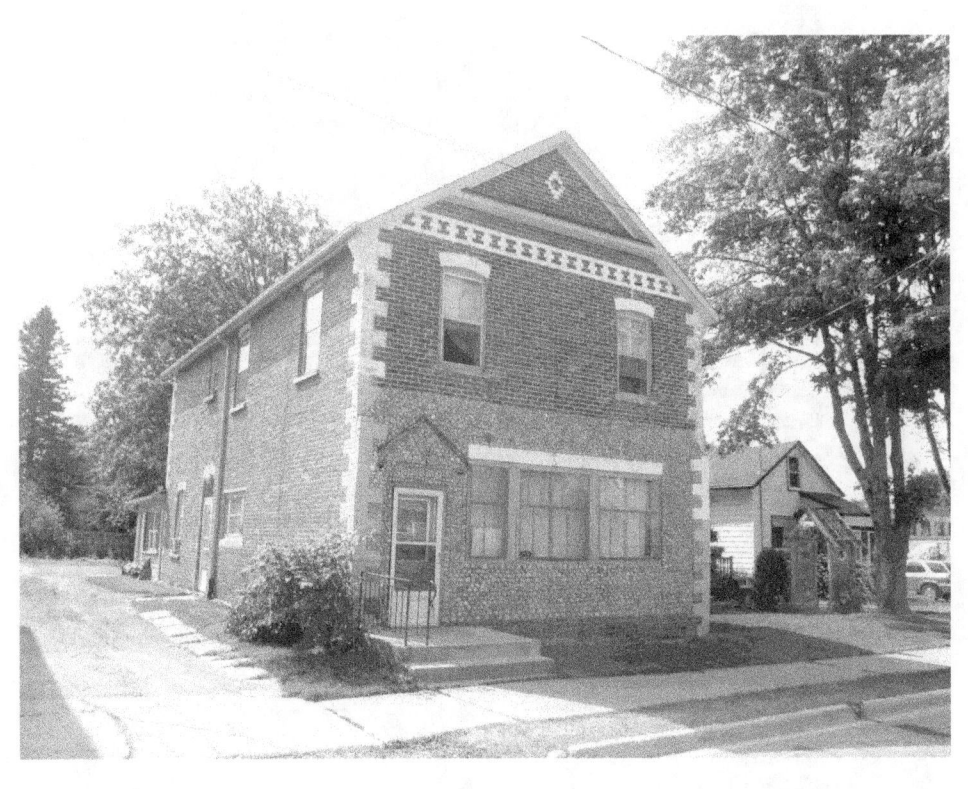

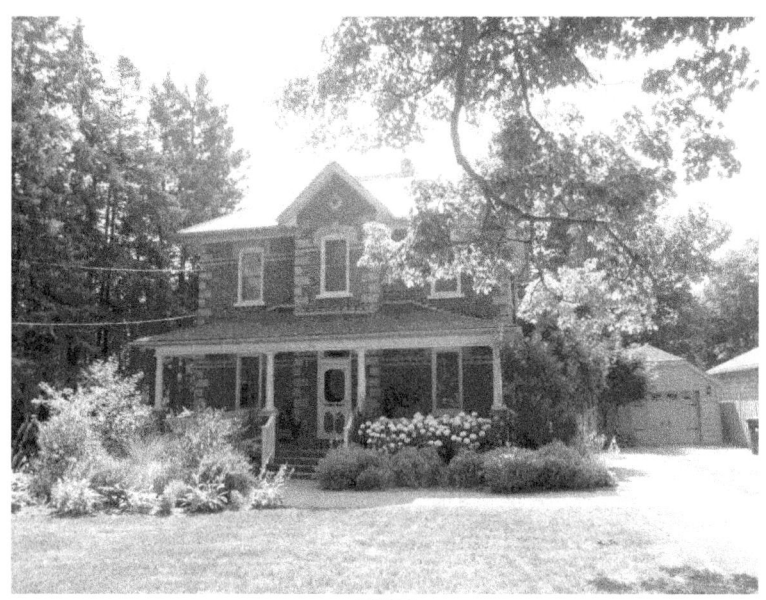

#201

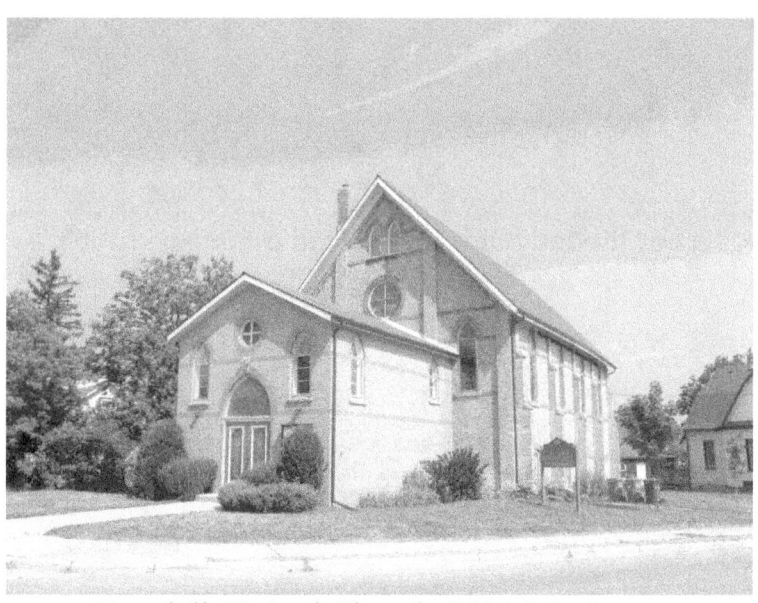

Dundalk United Church, 200 Main Street

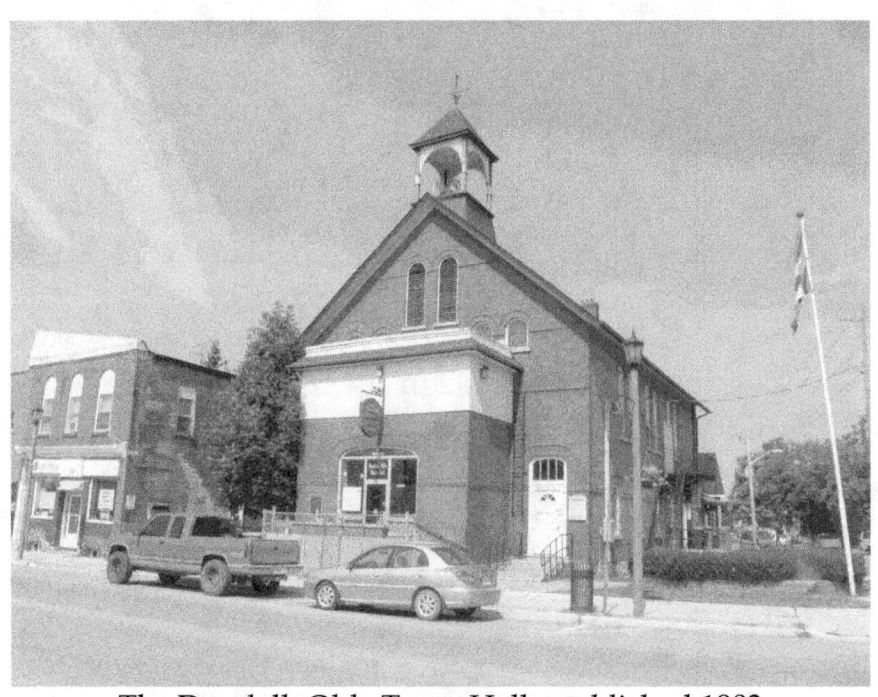

The Dundalk Olde Town Hall established 1903

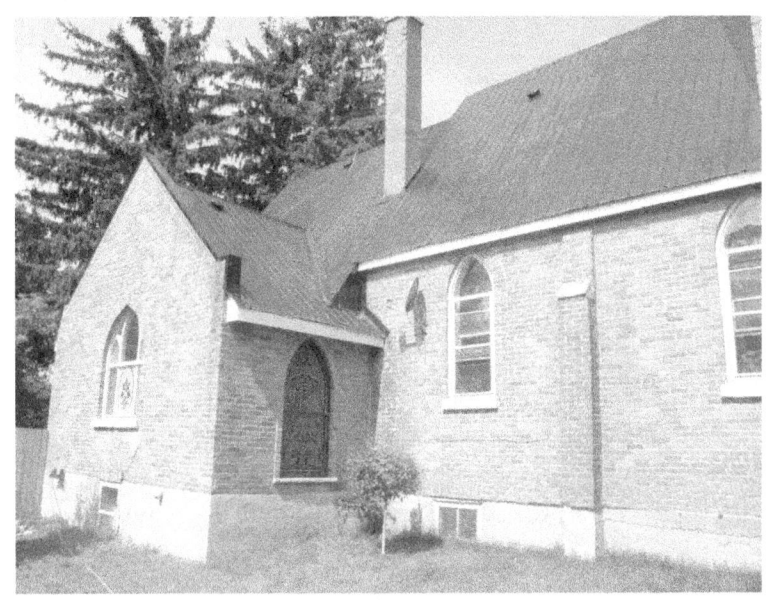

Former St. James Anglican Church – 1923
31 Artemesia Street

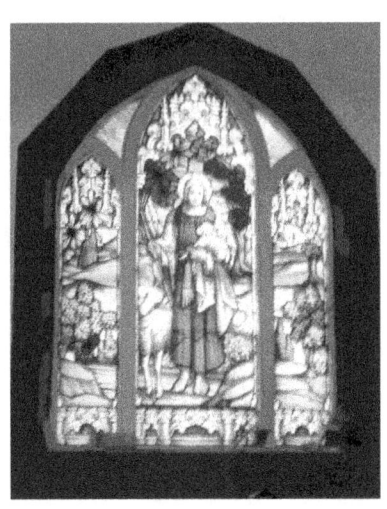

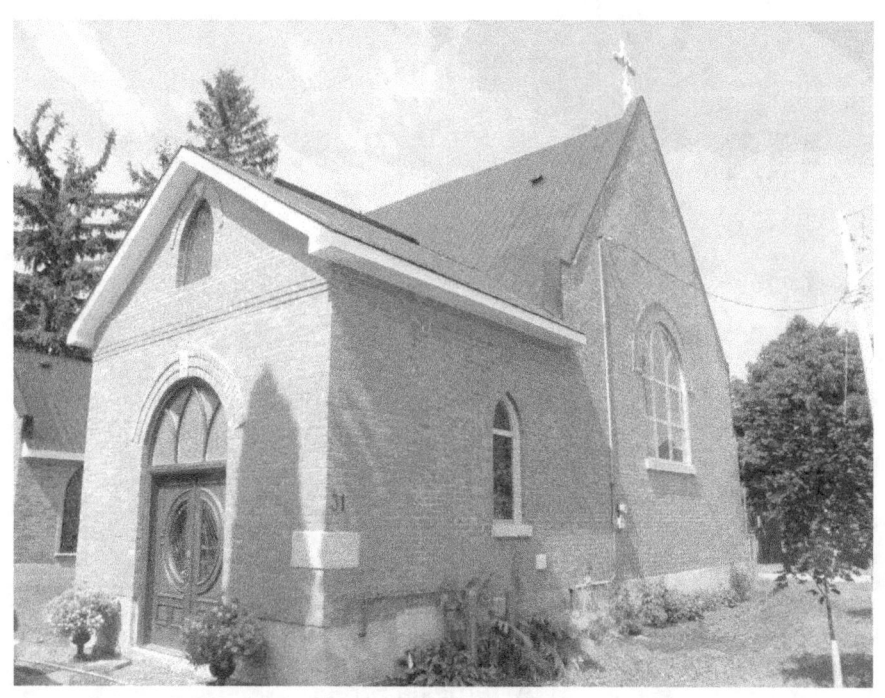

St. James Anglican Church converted to a home

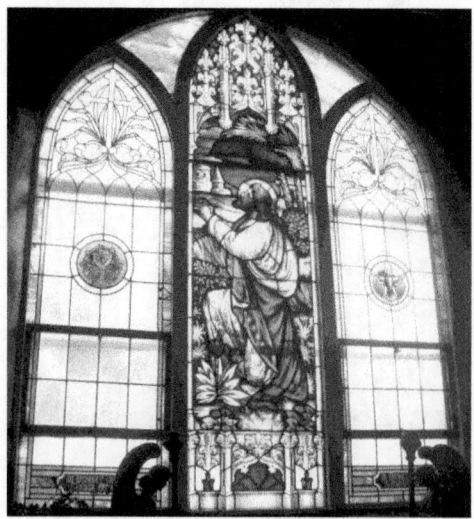

Stained glass windows

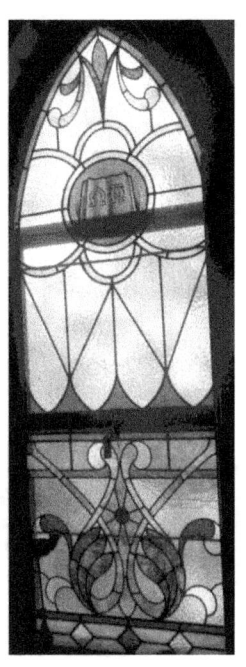

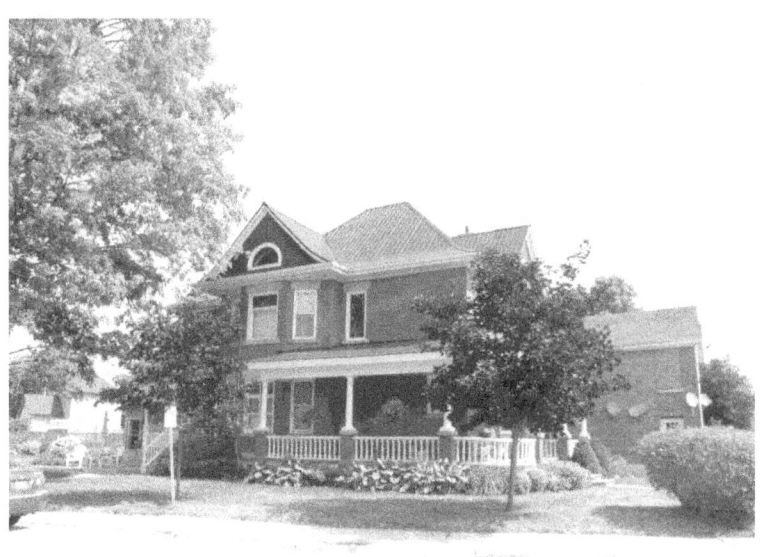

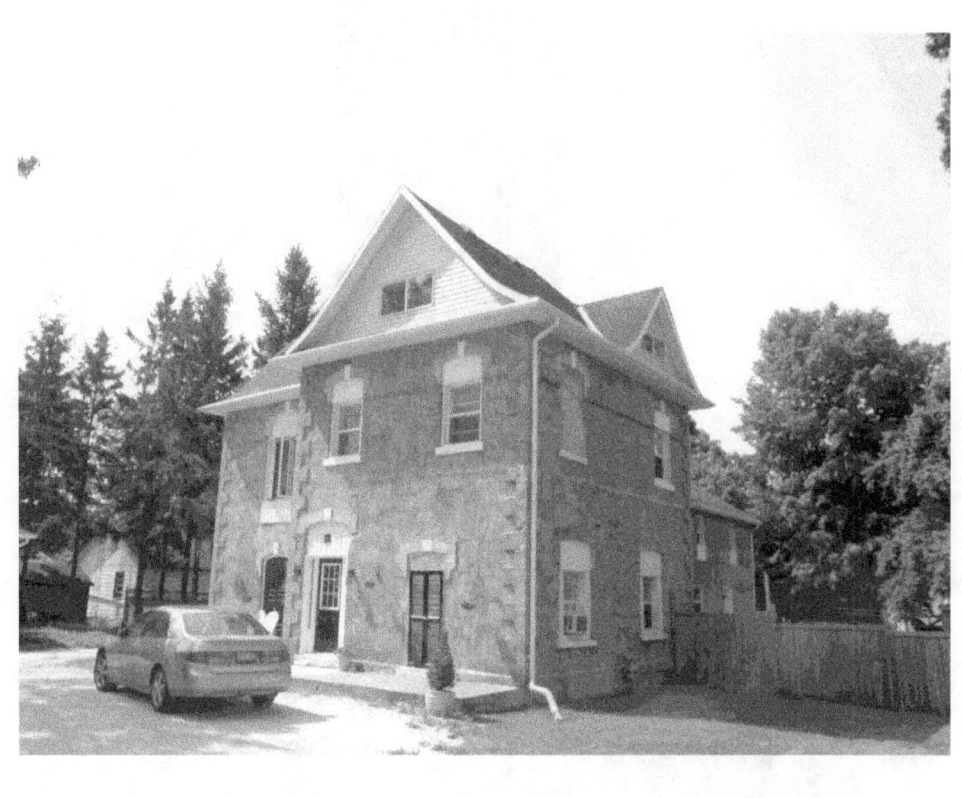